AVATAR

THE LAST AIRBENDER.

CREATED BY

BRYAN KONIETZKO

MICHAEL DANTE DIMARTINO

LEGACY

TEXT BY MICHAEL TEITELBAUM

ORIGINAL ILLUSTRATIONS BY STEVE AHN & DAN PARSONS

COLORS BY WES DZIOBA

INSIGHT ⬡ EDITIONS

San Rafael, California

Dear Tenzin,

As I begin to put this book together for you, you are five years old. Though you are still a boy, every day you are becoming bigger, smarter, and stronger. There might come a time, oh, say, between the ages of 13 and 25, when you'll be too busy with your friends, your studies, your training, or girls to listen to your old man. So let me say this while your ears and heart are still open: Through hard work, love, and friendship, you can accomplish anything. Maybe even save the world.

The most important thing you can learn is who you are, but you can't truly know yourself until you understand where you came from. I think the time has come to give you a sense of your history—our history—because it is an important one.

I would not be here—and you certainly wouldn't be here!—if it weren't for the amazing journey that I took with your mother, your Uncle Sokka, and our dear friend, Toph. This book is a collection of stories and mementos from that time in my life. Your mom, Sokka, Toph, and I made it just for you. This isn't every single detail. You'll learn those things in school. It's just a few of the more meaningful moments.

I know you won't be able to understand a lot of this for years to come, but one fact is of great magnitude, and the sooner you understand it, the better: You are the first Airbender to be born in more than one hundred years, and one day you will lead the Air Nation. For now, unless your mom and I bring you an Airbender brother or sister—it looks like it's just you and me, kid!

Every Avatar in history has had a role in shaping the state of the world. But the things that happened during my life as the Avatar—especially during the days when I had to learn waterbending, earthbending, and firebending on the run—shaped history as none before.

I hope this book gives you some insight into my life and the world as you know it today.

I may be the Avatar, but no human lives forever. When my time is over, the spirit of the Avatar will live on and eventually return in another. It will be up to you to train the next Avatar. I want you to know all you can before these responsibilities fall upon you.

Enjoy this book, my son, and know that your mother and I will always be proud of you.

With love,
Dad

群市

THE WATER TRIBES

The people of the Water Tribes are split between the North and South Poles. They have cultural differences, but both are accustomed to living in cold, snowy places.

善

MAP *of the* WORLD

BEFORE I TELL YOU about our world, its peoples, traditions, and customs, it's important that you have a sense of place—an understanding of where all of these events happened. There's a lot you can learn just from studying maps.

火烈

THE FIRE NATION

The Fire Nation is located on a group of volcanic islands around the equator. It is a hot, barren land. The Fire Nation has always been very powerful and technologically advanced, and when I was young, the Fire Nation conquered the other three nations in a brutal war.

天下

THE EARTH KINGDOM

The Earth Kingdom is the biggest of the four nations. It takes up an entire continent. It also has the most people. This is where your Auntie Toph is from.

THE AIR NOMADS

The Air Nomads were my people. One day, when we're both ready, I'll tell you how they were lost—all except for me.

THE AVATAR

AS YOU ALREADY KNOW, the Avatar can bend all four elements. The spirits give the Avatar the powerful ability to master all four elements through earthbending, firebending, waterbending, and airbending. An Avatar's mission in this world is to maintain balance among the four elements and help bring balance, peace, and prosperity to the four nations.

THE AVATAR STATE

The Avatar before me was Avatar Roku, and he taught me that when the Avatar enters the Avatar State, that Avatar is at his or her most powerful . . . but also the most vulnerable. For me, it is anger or fear that sends me into the Avatar State. My bending becomes overwhelming, and I can take on entire armies. But at the same time, I risk hurting innocent people, as that much power can be a dangerous thing.

In the Avatar State, I am in touch with the power and energy of all my past lives—every Avatar who ever lived. Which is great! Except that if an Avatar dies in the Avatar State, the Avatar cycle will end . . . forever.

Some great Avatars from the past include:

AVATAR ROKU
(A FIREBENDER)

AVATAR KYOSHI
(AN EARTHBENDER)

AVATAR KURUK
(A WATERBENDER)

THE UNBROKEN LINE

I am the Avatar . . . at least, right now. I am just the latest physical incarnation of that spirit. But I get to share some of the memories, experiences, and sometimes even advice of all the other Avatars who have ever lived. When the physical form of an Avatar dies, the Avatar Spirit is reborn. The Avatar cycle never changes: Fire, Air, Water, Earth.

THE HUNDRED YEAR WAR

THE HUNDRED YEAR WAR changed the whole world. I wasn't around to prevent it when I should have been, and so stopping it became the defining mission of my life. I'm telling you this because I want you to understand the profound impact each life choice you make has not only on you, but on the people around you. This graphic history was created to teach children about the Hundred Year War and its importance in our shared history. I saved it for many years, and now I can finally share it with you.

Long ago, in the Fire Nation, Prince Sozin, heir to the throne of the Fire Lord, was best friends with a Firebender named Roku.

NICE MOVE, SOZIN!

Years later, Sozin became Fire Lord, and Roku was revealed to be the Avatar.

OUR NATION IS ENJOYING AN UNPRECEDENTED TIME OF PEACE AND WEALTH. WE SHOULD SHARE THIS PROSPERITY WITH THE REST OF THE WORLD.

WHERE ARE YOU GOING WITH THIS?

IT IS TIME WE EXPAND THIS EMPIRE!

NO! THE FOUR NATIONS MUST REMAIN SEPARATE. THIS IS THE LAST I WANT TO HEAR ABOUT THIS!

IN TIME, THE FIRE NATION WILL BE UNSTOPPABLE!

But Sozin did not listen to his old friend. He began building up the Fire Nation army and navy.

THE HUNDRED
YEAR WAR

Years later, when Roku's home was threatened by a volcanic eruption, Sozin came to help. However, once Roku was trapped by a gas geyser, Sozin left him to die.

WITH ROKU GONE, THERE IS NO ONE TO OPPOSE ME!

Twelve years later, a comet streaked across the sky, giving Sozin and his fellow firebenders nearly unlimited power.

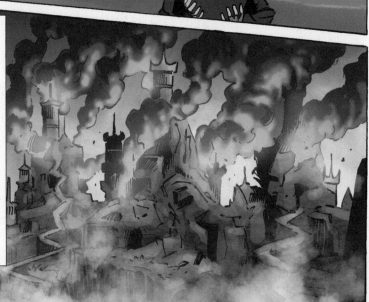

Sozin used this power to launch his attack. He started by destroying the Air Nomads, knowing that the next Avatar would be an Airbender, and aware that only the Avatar could stop him.

What he didn't know was that when Aang had learned he was the Avatar, he had run away from home, daunted by the responsibility.

Next, Sozin began his invasion of the Earth Kingdom.

Then came attacks on the Water Tribes. Although the icy terrain of the North Pole prevented the Fire Nation from taking over the North, the Southern Water Tribes were greatly weakened by constant raids.

I AM FIRE LORD! I HAVE ALL POWERS AND ALL RIGHTS!

Years later, when Sozin died, his son, Azulon became the new Fire Lord and continued the invasion of the Earth Kingdom…

…and set up many Fire Nation colonies in the Earth Kingdom.

STOP SLOWING DOWN! NO BREAKS!

In the 95th year of the war, Azulon died, and his son, Ozai was crowned the new Fire Lord. By the 99th year, the Fire Nation had wiped out the Air Nomads, almost destroyed the Water Tribes, and controlled most of the Earth Kingdom. It appeared their victory was close at hand.

Then, as the war entered its 100th year, something amazing happened. A Waterbender named Katara and her brother Sokka found a 12-year-old boy and a sky bison frozen in an iceberg!

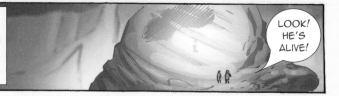

LOOK! HE'S ALIVE!

Aang turned out to be the last Airbender, and also the Avatar! He had survived the Fire Nation war against the Air Nomads. He was the last hope of stopping the Fire Nation from conquering the entire world. The Fire Nation knew that Aang was alive and planned to capture him. Ozai's exiled son, Prince Zuko, was determined to find the Avatar to regain his honor. As the Avatar, Aang needed to be trained in all four bending disciplines.

FEEL THE BENDING ENERGY FLOW THROUGH YOU . . . LIKE WATER.

Katara taught him waterbending.

GROUND YOURSELF, TWINKLE TOES!

In Earth Kingdom they met Toph, who became Aang's earthbending teacher and a part of what Sokka named "Team Avatar."

YOU MUST DIRECT THE FLAME TO AVOID GETTING BURNED.

Later, Prince Zuko changed sides, joined Team Avatar, and taught Aang Firebending.

When the comet that had given Sozin his power returned, Fire Lord Ozai started his final attack in the Earth Kingdom.

THE TIME HAS COME FOR OUR FINAL VICTORY!

Aang knew that he would have to face the Fire Lord. He met a Lion Turtle who gave him some wisdom but struggled with the idea of such extreme conflict. As an Air Nomad, he had been schooled in the ways of peace and harmony, not war and destruction.

THE TRUE MIND CAN WEATHER ALL THE LIES AND ILLUSIONS WITHOUT BEING LOST.

THE TRUE HEART CAN TOUGH THE POISON OF HATRED WITHOUT BEING HARMED.

Aang squared off in a final battle with Fire Lord Ozai. Using the mystical knowledge provided by the Lion Turtle, Aang removed the Fire Lord's bending ability.

I HAVE SPARED YOUR LIFE, BUT YOU NO LONGER HAVE ANY POWER.

Team Avatar

I DIDN'T END the Hundred Year War all by myself—I feel proud and grateful to have had help from friends throughout my journey. The deep bonds forged during that time will last for the rest of my life, and I'm so happy to see that the people who helped me along the way have been celebrated as heroes since the war ended.

KATARA

Your mother, Katara, grew up as the sole Waterbender in the Southern Water Tribe. After her mother was lost in a Fire Nation raid and her father left to fight in the Hundred Year War, she was forced to grow up quickly, developing into a maternal figure in the village.

Everything changed when she and Sokka discovered me in the iceberg. After they brought me to the Northern Water Tribe so that both Katara and I could learn from a waterbending master, they decided to accompany me on my journey. When I was badly injured by lightning in a battle, it was Katara who healed me and saved my life.

Katara played a vital part in the pivotal battle of the Hundred Year War, healing Zuko when he took a blast to the chest and going up against Princess Azula herself.

After the war, Katara and I began dating, and, of course, we eventually got married and had you, Kya, and Bumi.

SOKKA

As you know, your Uncle Sokka is one of my best friends. As the Southern Water Tribe's oldest male once all the warriors left to fight in the Hundred Year War, Sokka became the leader of the tribe at a young age. He protected the village and trained children in defense.

Although he doesn't have any bending skills, Sokka was just as important to Team Avatar as the rest of us. He is a master strategist whose ingenious plans got us out of many tight spots. Not to mention that his skill with a boomerang is legendary. And, in the Fire Nation, Sokka was trained by a master swordsman, Piandao, and learned how to forge his own sword out of a meteorite.

Toward the end of the Hundred Year War, Sokka was happily reunited with his father, a formidable warrior who Sokka had always looked up to.

TOPH

Blind since birth, Toph Beifong became the most skilled Earthbender in the world. She even invented a new variety of earthbending along the way—metalbending. Toph was my earthbending mentor and beyond that was an indispensable part of Team Avatar.

Toph grew up as the sheltered only child of the aristocratic Beifong family. Because they were ashamed of her blindness, her parents kept her hidden away. But it was in the caves that she mastered earthbending, under the guidance of the blind badgermoles that dwelled there. With her great skills, Toph—under the moniker "The Blind Bandit"—secretly became the champion of an underground earthbending tournament. That was where we found her and convinced her to become my instructor. In the end, she decided to leave her old life behind to travel with us and help us take down the Fire Nation.

ZUKO

Although Prince Zuko started as an enemy, he ultimately joined our cause, becoming my firebending teacher, as well as a valuable ally and beloved friend.

When we first met him, Zuko had been exiled from the Fire Nation by Fire Lord Ozai and tasked with capturing me to restore his honor and birthright to the throne. Accompanied by his uncle Iroh, he pursued Team Avatar relentlessly. But, eventually, Ozai became unhappy with Zuko interfering with his conquest plans and sent his sister, Princess Azula, to capture him and Iroh.

Later, Zuko decided to join our side and help me restore peace to our world. Together, we rediscovered the long-lost original Firebenders, the dragons.

After the war, Zuko was crowned Fire Lord, and over the years we have worked together to establish harmony amongst the nations.

THE AIR NOMADS

THE AIR NOMADS were a peaceful, spiritual people who lived in harmony with nature. Because we moved around a lot, our flag was really important to us. It symbolized that despite the distance among us, we were one nation. The swirling circle represents the wind.

THE SOUTHERN AIR TEMPLE

This is where I lived as a child, and where Monk Gyatso taught me airbending . . . and so much more. He taught me to respect all life and helped shape the man I am today. I still miss him.

The inner sanctuary of the temple houses statues of past Avatars. The temple also has an airball arena, where I got to play one of my favorite games with other Airbenders. The Southern Air Temple is where I found my pal Momo.

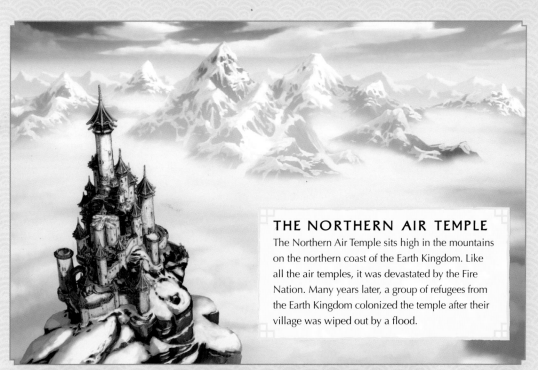

THE NORTHERN AIR TEMPLE

The Northern Air Temple sits high in the mountains on the northern coast of the Earth Kingdom. Like all the air temples, it was devastated by the Fire Nation. Many years later, a group of refugees from the Earth Kingdom colonized the temple after their village was wiped out by a flood.

THE EASTERN AIR TEMPLE

This temple holds a special place in my heart. Before the war, it was one of the places where Airbenders got to choose the sky bison they would be with throughout their lives. This is where I met Appa. He was at my side during all the trials and adventures of my youth, and is still my loyal companion.

THE WESTERN AIR TEMPLE

Of the four air temples, the Western Air Temple is the most unusual. It is located in a mountain range north of the Fire Nation. Instead of rising up from a mountain, it actually sticks down from the bottom of a cliff! It is full of lots of beautiful paintings of sky bison.

THE SOUTHERN AIR TEMPLE

IT MAKES ME sad that you will never get to see the Southern Air Temple as it was when I was your age. You can just imagine how special it was to experience its beauty in person.

THE MAIN SANCTUARY

Inside the main sanctuary the monks led group meditation sessions, deepening the spiritual quests of Air Nomads. Behind a thick wooden door was the sanctuary's statue room, which contained statues of every Avatar who ever lived. No key exists. The door can only be opened using airbending.

When I visited the Southern Air Temple, I found it deserted. No one had lived there for a very long time. I used airbending to enter the temple's inner sanctuary, where I saw statues of many of the great Avatars of the past. I recognized one statue as Avatar Roku, the Firebender who was Avatar before me, even though no one had ever told me his name. Somehow I just knew. The statues were arranged in the order of the Avatar Cycle: Fire, Air, Water, Earth. Seeing the inner sanctuary was amazing, but my trip to the Southern Air Temple was also sad. At that time, I really was the last Airbender.

AIRBENDERS

WHAT IS AIRBENDING?

Tenzin, I can already tell that one of the greatest joys of my life will be training you in airbending so you can fully realize the amazing gift we share. Of course, you have already experienced many of the physical, mental, and spiritual sensations all Airbenders feel.

As you know, airbending is one of the four elemental bending arts. In time, as you study and practice, you'll learn to control air currents, either for gliding or to use as a tool or defensive weapon. As General Iroh once said to Prince Zuko: "Air is the element of freedom."

SEASON: AUTUMN

Each element has a season that gives the benders of that element increased power. Autumn is the season of Airbenders. Back when there were lots of Air Nomads, more Air Nomad children were born during autumn than during any other season.

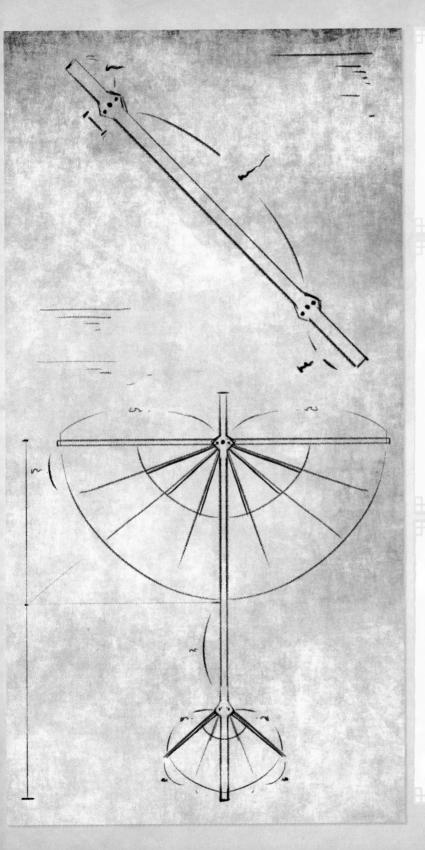

AIRBENDING STAFF/GLIDER

Our wooden staffs open up into gliders, which allow us to catch air currents and fly. A major part of Air Nomad culture, these staffs had the added bonus of giving us the ability to implement complex airbending techniques.

THE MONKS

Air Nomads were led by an order of monks. They taught future generations how to become Airbenders. I have explained to you how Monk Gyatso was my teacher, but he was also the only father I ever really had. He cared for me as if I were his own son, and his death at the hands of the Fire Nation was what drove me to stop the Fire Nation and restore peace to the world.

PHILOSOPHY

It gives me such pleasure and satisfaction to pass along to you the philosophy that Monk Gyatso taught me when I was your age. I give to you our deep belief in peace and harmony, honesty and ethical behavior. Along with these gifts, my son, comes the lifelong striving for spiritual enlightenment. As I have already taught you, the taking of any life is against our core beliefs. That is why we are strict vegetarians.

THE WATER TRIBES

ORIGINALLY, THERE WAS only one Water Tribe, located at the North Pole. Eventually, a group of warriors, Waterbenders, and healers established a new tribe at the South Pole. However, the Hundred Year War disrupted contact between the two tribes, so when the Southern Water Tribe was suffering from brutal raids, the Northern Water Tribe was unable to help. The Water Tribe flag depicts a circle with a crescent moon and ocean waves representing the Moon Spirit and the Ocean Spirit, who give the Water Tribes their powers and philosophy.

THE NORTHERN WATER TRIBE

The Northern Water Tribe is a very sophisticated culture. They live in a huge city made of ice and complicated waterway systems. The only way into the city is through a gateway controlled by Waterbenders. This ingenuity helped protect the Northern Water Tribe from being conquered by the Fire Nation during the war.

People in the North tend to live a strict, formal lifestyle. In the old days, only boys could train to become Waterbenders—the girls had to become healers. But your mother changed all of that. She wasn't going to let anyone tell her what she could or couldn't do!

FOGGY SWAMP TRIBE

Members of the Foggy Swamp Tribe live in a
settlement in the Earth Kingdom. Amazingly, the
people of the Southern and Northern Water Tribes
didn't even know these Waterbenders existed
until your mother and I found them by accident.
They can make vines move by bending the water
flowing through the plants.

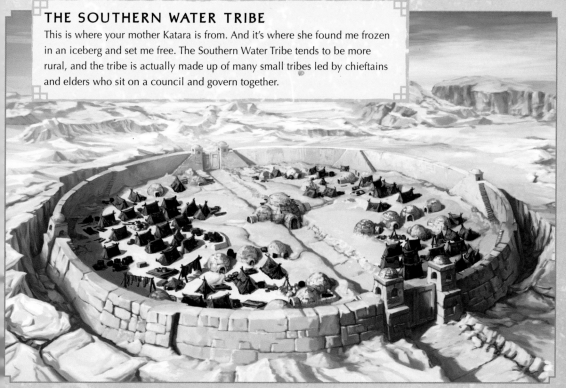

THE SOUTHERN WATER TRIBE

This is where your mother Katara is from. And it's where she found me frozen
in an iceberg and set me free. The Southern Water Tribe tends to be more
rural, and the tribe is actually made up of many small tribes led by chieftains
and elders who sit on a council and govern together.

WATERBENDERS

WHAT IS WATERBENDING?

Waterbending is the art of controlling and manipulating water in all its forms. The moon was the first Waterbender, pushing and pulling the ocean tides. I learned to waterbend from your mother. I understood how the flow of chi was crucial to this style of bending. It was thrilling to hone this talent.

SEASON: WINTER

Winter is the dominant season for Waterbenders. More Waterbenders are born during the winter than during any other season.

PHILOSOPHY

Waterbending focuses on using another's energy against them, allowing their defense to become their offense. Their movements are fluid and graceful, working with the environment to utilize defensive techniques as attacks without directly harming their opponents.

HEALING POWERS

Some Waterbenders—like your mother—can use their waterbending abilities to help heal a sick or injured person.

BLOODBENDING

The dark side of waterbending is bloodbending, which only high-level benders can do. Some Waterbenders can manipulate the blood and other bodily fluids of another person, controlling the person's movements. It is a horrific way to force people to do things against their will, and your mother fought hard to ensure that it would be treated as a criminal act.

THE MOON AND OCEAN SPIRITS

ONE OF THE MOST ASTOUNDING and deeply spiritual places I visited was the Spirit Oasis at the North Pole. There I learned about the Moon and Ocean Spirits and how they give Waterbenders their power. In the middle of all that cold and ice was this lush, tropical clearing with a small pond. There were two koi in the pond. The white koi with the black spot was Tui, the physical embodiment of the Moon Spirit. The black koi with the white spot was La, the physical form of the Ocean Spirit.

The balance between Tui and La—between the moon and the ocean—fuels the abilities of Waterbenders. These spirits are part of every Waterbender, and as the son of a Waterbender, Tenzin, they are also part of you.

In order to stop the Fire Nation's navy when they attacked the Northern Water Tribe, I went into the Avatar State and merged with La, the Ocean Spirit. Together, we managed to defeat Admiral Zhao and the Fire Nation Navy. In this union, I felt as powerful as I have ever felt, but as with every time I enter the Avatar State, there is a component of feeling enraged and out of control. I did what I felt I had to do at the time, but I was glad when it was over. I always feel exhausted and relieved when I come out of the Avatar State.

PRINCESS YUE'S SACRIFICE

Princess Yue of the Northern Water Tribe was saved by the Moon Spirit when she was a baby. After Admiral Zhao killed Tui, the Moon Spirit, Yue knew that she had to repay her debt. She sacrificed her own life, bringing Tui back to life and becoming the Moon Spirit.

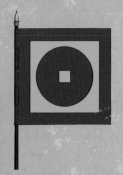

THE EARTH KINGDOM

THE PEOPLE OF the Earth Kingdom are proud and strong. They believe in working with the other nations of the world while upholding their many longtime traditions. Their cities are grand examples of a civilized culture working together for the common good. The kingdom is ruled by a monarchy, under a king or queen. The Earth Kingdom flag is a square containing a circle that houses a smaller square, which represents the many layers of deep rock that make up the Earth Kingdom, as well as the depth of the power of its people.

BA SING SE

Ba Sing Se is the largest city in the entire world. The city is surrounded by two enormous walls. The gates to these walls can only be opened by a team of Earthbenders. Between the two walls is where most of the food for the city is grown. Inside the inner wall is where the city itself is located.

The metropolis of the inner city is divided into "rings" by class, and the massive Earth Kingdom palace sits at the heart of the city.

During the war, Ba Sing Se and the Earth Kingdom were secretly ruled by the Dai Li, a clandestine police force that had become so corrupt and influential that they reduced the Earth King to a mere figurehead and turned the city over to the Fire Nation.

OMASHU

The second largest city in the Earth Kingdom is Omashu, which was once ruled by my dear friend King Bumi. He was a great leader. I have fond memories of when we were both children, sliding down the city's mail chutes and ramps. As an adult, he was a key ally in my quest to rid the world of Fire Nation oppression.

KYOSHI ISLAND

One of my predecessors as Avatar was a powerful earthbending woman named Kyoshi. The island on which she was born more than four hundred years ago is now named after her. A group of powerful warriors called the Kyoshi Warriors defend the island.

GAOLING

The city of Gaoling is where Toph is from and where we met her at an earthbending tournament. Master Yu's Earthbending Academy is also in Gaoling. Master Yu is another great master and teacher of earthbending.

EARTHBENDERS

WHAT IS EARTHBENDING?

Earthbending is the ability to manipulate the earth in all its forms, such as rocks or dirt. Earthbenders tend to be very strong and muscular. When I learned earthbending from Toph—which was not easy—I remember feeling like my muscles were becoming part of the rocks I was moving. As the rocks I practiced with got harder and heavier, I could feel my muscles getting stronger.

GROUP EARTHBENDING

Earthbenders can combine their power to accomplish amazing feats. Working as a team, a group of Earthbenders can raise a huge section of earth to form a wall. They can team up to lift rocks, dirt, or coal into the air while others propel the material forward.

SEASON: SPRING

The season of the Earthbenders is Spring. It is the time when many living things on Earth are reborn, growing up from the ground, which the Earthbenders control. The power of Earthbenders increases during the spring, and more Earthbenders are born during spring than during any other season.

SANDBENDING

Sandbending is a special form of earthbending practiced by Earthbenders who live in the desert. Sandbenders can use bending to make the tiny grains form solid projectiles or to gain firmer footing on the loose, shifting sands.

METALBENDING

For thousands of years, people (even Earthbenders themselves) believed that it was impossible for Earthbenders to use their bending powers to bend metal. But when Toph was kidnapped and imprisoned in a metal cage, she sensed the original minerals inside the refined metal and invented metalbending.

PHILOSOPHY

Earthbenders are proud and strong. They believe in peaceful coexistence and cooperation with the other nations of the world. They use their bending abilities for defense and to power their industries.

WELCOME *to the* JASMINE DRAGON

ALTHOUGH GENERAL IROH of the Fire Nation was a decorated military hero, it turned out that he loved tea much more than he loved war. Iroh became a good friend, and I always enjoy visiting his tea shop in Ba Sing Se. In fact, one of the most important moments of my life took place right out in front of the Jasmine Dragon. It was there that your mother and I shared the kiss that began our relationship. Although it was years ago, I remember it like it was yesterday. And it still makes me smile.

THE KYOSHI WARRIORS

THE KYOSHI WARRIORS are a team of female fighters named after Avatar Kyoshi, an Earthbender who was the Avatar just before Roku. Avatar Kyoshi originally put this team of elite warriors together to protect her homeland, Kyoshi Island. She used her metal fans as weapons. The Kyoshi Warriors adopted these weapons, as well as her costume, makeup, and fighting style. When we were young, the Kyoshi Warriors were led by Suki, and your Uncle Sokka was smitten.

TY LEE has helped me out many times, but she didn't start out on our side. As a teenager, she ran away from home and joined a Fire Nation Circus. Before she joined the Kyoshi Warriors, Ty Lee had teamed up with Princess Azula and helped her try to destroy me. As a Kyoshi Warrior, Ty Lee practices Chi Blocking, a martial arts technique that attacks pressure points in the human body and blocks one's chi, leaving its victim temporarily paralyzed.

SUKI
is the leader of
the Kyoshi Warriors. She
began her training when she
was just eight years old. She
had skills that your Uncle Sokka
could only have dreamed of,
and they were an amazing
team together.

DEAR TENZIN,

Well, kid, here it goes. Your father, Twinkle Toes, asked me to give you a story about him. And so I thought you would like to hear about the first time I ever showed your dad who's boss around here. Since I know how much kids love seeing stories come to life in pictures, I asked an artist friend of mine to draw a little story for you. Here it is:

I used to compete in earthbending tournaments as the Blind Bandit. Oh, man, I sure was the best. Nobody could beat me—not even "The Boulder."

THE BOULDER FEELS CONFLICTED ABOUT FIGHTING A YOUNG, BLIND GIRL!

Beating that guy was a piece of cake. Hey, what else would you expect from the champion?

I OFFER A SACK OF GOLD TO ANYONE WHO CAN BEAT THE BLIND BANDIT!

I WILL! I'LL GET INTO THE RING WITH THE BLIND BANDIT!

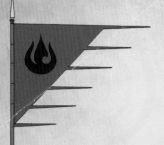

THE FIRE NATION

THE FIRE NATION is located on a group of volcanic islands, many of which are still active. It was once the world leader in technological advancements and industry, but prosperity didn't spread to all of its citizens. Fire Lords Sozin, Azulon, and Ozai were responsible for the Hundred Year War, but Zuko and I believe the Fire Nation can correct its past.

The Fire Nation flag contains their national emblem, a teardrop-shaped flame in the center of a triangular banner.

FIRE NATION RESOURCES

Skilled craftsmen use fire to help build fortresses, ships, weapons, and all things metal. The Fire Nation's hot climate and excellent volcanic ash also make it great for growing food like cabbages, lychee nuts, and some of the world's best tea. I'm a fan of their spicier dishes, like fire cakes and flaming fire flakes.

THE FIRE FESTIVAL

This is a traveling street fair that moves from village to village. People at the fair wear hand-carved masks, and vendors sell all kinds of local foods and handmade crafts. You can see puppet shows, magicians, jugglers, fireworks, and all kinds of amazing firebending demonstrations.

THE FIRE NATION CAPITAL

The Capital City is one of the largest cities in the world. It is located on an island in the western part of the Fire Nation. Its huge harbor is large enough to hold twelve Empire-class warships. The city is home to the Fire Nation Royal Palace and the government of the Fire Nation.

FIREBENDERS

WHAT IS FIREBENDING?

Of all four bending arts, firebending is the most aggressive and offense-oriented. The manipulation of fire is controlled through breathing. The more skilled I got at firebending, the more I felt my hot breath fueling my hands and feet as they channeled the flames I was bending. All Firebenders draw their power from the sun. Some powerful Firebenders even have the ability to generate and redirect lightning, which requires a level of inner peace. The first human Firebenders learned the technique from dragons, the original Firebenders.

SEASON: SUMMER

Summer is the most dominant season for Firebenders. At night, their powers decrease. Firebenders also get weaker during solar eclipses and full moons.

AGNI KAI

A duel between two Firebenders, usually fought at sunset.

PHILOSOPHY

The Fire Nation is a mysterious and aggressive society. For generations, an all-powerful Fire Lord dominated his people, who lived in fear. I needed every ounce of my courage to confront him during the war. Since the war, Fire Lord Zuko has worked hard to change the pattern of ruling through intimidation.

THE FIRE NATION ROYAL FAMILY TREE

THE HISTORY OF THE FIRE NATION ROYAL FAMILY is filled with conflict, betrayal, and a hunger for power so great that some even resorted to despicable acts to advance their status. And since understanding the past is one way to avoid mistakes in the future, here's a family tree to help you keep it all straight.

FIRE LORD OZAI

FIRE LORD SOZIN

FIRE LORD AZULON

IROH

❖ Used a comet to enhance his army's firebending powers to launch the attack against the Air Nomads.
❖ Started the Hundred Year War.

❖ Continued the war started by his father, Sozin. Won many battles in the Earth Kingdom. Almost completely destroyed the Southern Water Tribe.
❖ Poisoned by his son, Ozai.

❖ Crown prince of the Fire Nation but his brother Ozai was appointed Fire Lord instead.
❖ Fire Nation General
❖ Led the Siege of Ba Sing Se, where he was unsuccessful once his son, Lu Ten, died in that battle.
❖ Grand Lotus of the Order of the White Lotus

- Usurped his brother Iroh's birthright to the throne of the Fire Lord.
- Guilty of patricide.
- Banished his wife.
- Exiled his son.
- His defeat by Avatar Aang brought an end to the Hundred Year War.

URSA

- Forced to marry Ozai by Fire Lord Azulon.
- Banished from the Fire Nation by Fire Lord Ozai.

AZULA

- Named for her grandfather, Azulon.
- A firebending prodigy
- Defeated by her brother, Zuko, and placed in a mental health institution.

ZUKO

- Scarred and exiled from the Fire Kingdom by his father, Fire Lord Ozai.
- Helped the Avatar to restore balance and end the war.
- Crowned Fire Lord at the end of the Hundred Year War.

THE BOY IN THE ICEBERG

WHILE MY FRIENDS and I were trying to stop the Hundred Year War, we stopped at Ember Island—the vacation home of Zuko's family—and discovered that a theater troupe there was putting on a play all about us! Of course we had to go see it, but it was really strange to see our lives being acted out on a stage. Or a version of our lives, anyway. To be honest, most of us didn't love the show or the way it told our story.

I was played by a girl—and kind of a goofy one. Not exactly flattering. Your mother came across as really bossy. Sokka's character only cared about food. On the other hand, Toph loved the big, beefy guy who played her! The play's ending upset me, too, since it had the Fire Lord winning. Fortunately, real life turned out differently. Here's the flyer announcing the play that we got when we went to see it.

HEY, TENZIN!

UNCLE SOKKA HERE. Aang asked me to share a story with you, so I thought I would tell you about one of the many times I singlehandedly saved the world. During the last battle of the Hundred Year War, while your dad was facing down Ozai, I was on a super important mission to take down the Fire Nation's fleet of airships.

We took out as many airships as we could to stop the Fire Nation's attack on the Earth Kingdom. At one point, there was a close call, though, where I truly got to prove my strength and courage!

When one of the enemy goons blasted us with fire, knocking us off of the airship, I used my sword to stop us from plummeting to the ground.

Due to my strength, fast thinking, and incredible reflexes, I saved us both!

Well . . . Okay, fine, Toph just reminded me that it was actually Suki who saved us in the end by crashing another airship into ours and giving us a surface to land upon. But I still stand by the fact that the entire war would have been lost if not for my ingenuity!

So take your wise Uncle Sokka's advice: Just because you can airbend doesn't mean you shouldn't build up your strategic skills and hone your reflexes. You never know when you'll need it!

WANTED

TENZIN, THERE'S SOMETHING else I want to tell you. My friends and I always believed that we were fighting for what was right. However, as you can see from these wanted posters, sometimes other people didn't agree with us, and so they ostracized us. I think history has borne out that we did the right thing, but you should remember that every story has at least two sides, and not everyone always agreed that we were the good guys. Time teaches you to be wiser and make better choices, and we had much to learn.

THE BLUE SPIRIT

TOPH BEIFONG

JEONG JEONG

IROH AND ZUKO

拿神　該逃犯身懷截氣神功
緝拏　能制起旋風飛遁如風
降　　捕者慎之慎之
　　　烈火君令

THE AVATAR

49

GAME TIME!

YOU KNOW, TENZIN, so much of what I've included in this book for you is serious, and maybe even sad or scary. But there were plenty of good moments on our adventures, too. Even fun ones! I never want you to lose sight of the importance of just having fun. When things start to get a little too serious, I've always loved to play games. Maybe you'll enjoy some of these, too!

AIR BALL
The object is to score points by shooting a ball into a goal. You can toss the ball into the goal or use airbending to guide it into the goal.

OTTER PENGUIN SLEDDING

One of the first things your mother and I ever did together was go penguin sledding at the South Pole! The rules are simple: hop on an otter penguin and slide down a snowy hill. Don't worry—the otter penguins love it too.

PAI SHO

Pai Sho is a game based on both strategy and chance that is played with round tiles on a circular board. Played by people of all ages, it has different variations and rules in each culture.

Before they became publicly known at the end of the Hundred Year War, members of the Order of the White Lotus—an ancient, secret society that transcends the boundaries of the four nations, and is interested only in philosophy, beauty, and truth—would use Pai Sho as a stealthy way to identify each other.

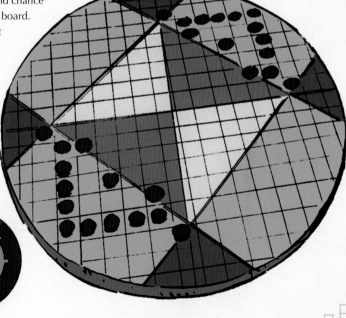

FIELD GUIDE TO LOCAL FAUNA

THE ANIMALS OF OUR WORLD are our friends and spiritual companions.
Here are some that I've encountered on my travels.

WHITE STRIPE
ON BACK

BADGERMOLE
Commonly found in: Earth Kingdom

WHITE PATCHES
ON FACE

WHISKERS

FURRY EARS

WIDE FLAT TAIL

KOALAOTTER
Commonly found in: Northern Water Tribe

POINTY SPINE

DRAGON-TYPE
WINGS

LARGE FIN ON BACK

50 FEET LONG

APPA AND MOMO

APPA AND MOMO have been my lifelong pals. They accompanied my friends and me on our adventures and sometimes even got into trouble on their own. Once I had to stop a buzzard wasp from taking Momo away. And Appa was kidnapped by Sandbenders and sold to a circus. After he escaped, he got captured again, this time by the Dai Li! In the end, Zuko rescued him, for which I will always be grateful.

I met Appa before the war, and he ended up in the ice along with me.

"Team Avatar" (Uncle Sokka came up with that name!)

Momo actually found me . . . at the Southern Air Temple when I was there with Katara and Sokka.

Momo wrapped himself around Sokka's head to scare me into the Avatar State. Winged lemurs are smart like that.

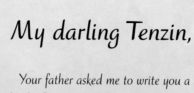

My darling Tenzin,

Your father asked me to write you a letter to include in this book of memories. I hope that when you're older and you look back on this letter and the rest of this book, you will feel the pride of your heritage and gain a deeper understanding of who you are and how you came to be the man you will grow into.

When I first met your father, he was a carefree boy, only occupied with having fun and playing games. Zooming down a snowy hill on the back of an otter penguin was of much greater concern to him than the weighty problems of a world torn apart by war.

Then he discovered that he was the Avatar. And when he awoke in our time, he blamed himself for the war, fearing that his choice to run away from his responsibilities had caused the horrors that descended upon our world—events he believed he could have prevented if only he had accepted his destiny.

One of the great joys of my life, and—I realized over the course of time—the thing that caused me to fall in love with your father, was watching him grow from the joyful, playful boy he was when I first met him to the amazing, thoughtful, powerful and wise man he became on his journey to accept his fate and embrace the power and responsibilities of being the Avatar.

I think what I loved the most about watching and being a part of your father's journey was that even as he gained wisdom and took on more responsibilities, he never lost his youthful joy and his love of games and jokes. I've never known anyone else who could be so serious about the important things in his life while at the same time embracing silliness so completely.

Throughout his life, your father not only had to carry the weight of being the Avatar, and of being the Avatar during the greatest crisis our world has ever faced, but he also had to shoulder the burden of being the last Airbender—the final surviving member of a proud and beautiful people. He carried that weight with him every day of his life, again blaming himself for not being there to help save his people.

And then you came along and everything changed—and not just in the way things change for every parent when a child is born. When we discovered that you too were an Airbender, and that the Airbenders would not die out with the passing of your father, we were filled with joy. A terrible burden was lifted from your father's shoulders, which only added to our happiness in welcoming you to our family.

The Airbenders' traditions will live on through you, and nothing could make your father and me happier and more proud. I look forward to watching you grow into manhood as I did with your father. And, unlike your father, you will have him there to guide your training every step of the way.

And so, my son, I wish for you the carefree joys of youth, the knowledge that comes with learning and experience, and the strength to accept and relish the power and responsibility of being an Airbender.

Your father and I will be there for you every step of the way. Know that we both will always love you very much.

Love,
Mom

THE SPIRIT WORLD

I DON'T WANT you to think that being the Avatar is only about power and fighting. I became Avatar during a war, but in peacetime Avatars spend their time in spiritual enlightenment. As with everything else I had to learn, I had to evolve spiritually in a hurry. Here are some of the things I've learned about the Spirit World.

THE PORTAL

The Spirit World was once part of our world, but thousands of years ago the portal between the Spirit World and our mortal world was closed. It is possible for me to pass between the two worlds, but only when I am in the Avatar State. That makes the journey very dangerous on a practical as well as a spiritual level.

THE LANDSCAPE

Certain places in the Spirit World appear like real, physical places you can walk in, with ground and trees and sky. Other parts of it are much harder to describe. They are more like feelings or thoughts than real places. It's the kind of thing that just can't be expressed in words.

THE FOG OF LOST SOULS

This region functions as a prison for humans banished from the mortal world. Once they enter the Fog, humans descend into madness and remain there for all eternity.

THE FINAL BATTLE

THE HUNDRED YEAR WAR finally came to an end when I defeated Fire Lord Ozai in a battle in the Earth Kingdom, but I couldn't have done it without the support and teamwork of my friends. Their courage, dedication, and skill helped turn what could have been the darkest moment of our history into a beacon of hope for our future.

At first, I tried to convince Ozai that we didn't have to fight and that together we could bring peace to the world. But he wanted no part of peace. We fought for a long time, and there were many close calls, but eventually I was able to enter the Avatar State. It was easy to overpower him then, but when the spirits of the past Avatars tried to deliver the finishing blow,

I regained control and exited the Avatar State. In the end, I chose to spare Ozai's life. I was taught by the monks to respect all life. Despite all the terrible things he was responsible for, I never wanted to kill the Fire Lord. Instead I removed his firebending ability so he could never use it to hurt anyone again. To this day, I'm still grateful that I was able to end the war without having to take a life. I want you to know, Tenzin, that there is always another way.

The end of the war marked the end of suffering for so many. After such a long period of strife, rebuilding our war-torn world was not without its obstacles, but a new era of peace began that day. I will always be proud of the part I played in that.

THE LION TURTLE

I CAN'T GIVE enough credit to the Lion Turtle for enlightening me to the ways of energybending just before I took on Fire Lord Ozai. He is an unsung hero of the Hundred Year War. Because of what he taught me, I was able to defeat Fire Lord Ozai without having to take his life.

The Lion Turtle is an enormous ancient being that has existed since the beginning of time itself. The Lion Turtle that helped me is the last of his kind. The rest were hunted and killed thousands of years before the Hundred Year War. The Lion Turtle has shared many wise words with me. I think this is a fitting place to end.

TO BEND ANOTHER'S ENERGY, YOUR OWN SPIRIT MUST BE UNBENDABLE, OR YOU WILL BE CORRUPTED AND DESTROYED.

IN THE ERA BEFORE THE AVATAR, WE BENT NOT THE ELEMENTS, BUT THE ENERGY WITHIN OURSELVES.

THE TRUE MIND CAN WEATHER ALL THE LIES AND ILLUSIONS WITHOUT BEING LOST.

THE TRUE HEART CAN TOUGH THE POISON OF HATRED WITHOUT BEING HARMED.

And so, dear Tenzin, I end this collection with the hope that you have enjoyed these stories, and with the strong wish that you learn from what I have shared with you here. May you use this information wisely.

Know that your mother and I love you so much—always.

I wish you a most peaceful (and fun) life, my son!

With much love,
Dad

INSIGHT EDITIONS

PO Box 3088
San Rafael, CA 94912
www.insighteditions.com

Find us on Facebook: www.facebook.com/InsightEditions
Follow us on Twitter: @insighteditions

Published by Insight Editions, San Rafael, California, in 2015.
No part of this book may be reproduced in any form
without written permission from the publisher.

Library of Congress Cataloging-in-Publication Data available.

ISBN: 978-1-60887-447-7

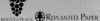

ROOTS of PEACE REPLANTED PAPER
Insight Editions, in association with Roots of Peace, will plant two
trees for each tree used in the manufacturing of this book. Roots of
Peace is an internationally renowned humanitarian organization
dedicated to eradicating land mines worldwide and converting
war-torn lands into productive farms and wildlife habitats. Roots
of Peace will plant two million fruit and nut trees in Afghanistan
and provide farmers there with the skills and support necessary
for sustainable land use.

Manufactured in China by Insight Editions

10 9 8 7 6 5 4 3 2 1

Publisher: Raoul Goff
Acquisitions Manager: Robbie Schmidt
Art Director: Chrissy Kwasnik
Designer: Jenelle Wagner
Executive Editor: Vanessa Lopez
Project Editor: Talia Platz and Ramin Zahed
Production Editor: Elaine Ou
Editorial Assistant: Katie DeSandro
Production Manager: Jane Chinn

nickelodeon
Senior Editor: Raina Moore
Sr. Art Director: James Salerno

Special thanks to Megan Casey, Brandon Hoang,
Sandra Pieloch, Katrin van Dam, and Kristen Yu-Um.